T0039956

NOTHING TO DECLARE

L'HISTOIRE DE
COLE

NOTHING
TO
DECLARE

HENRI
COLE

FARRAR STRAUS GIROUX

NEW YORK

FARRAR, STRAUS AND GIROUX

18 West 18th Street, New York 10011

First edition, 2015

Library of Congress Cataloging-in-Publication Data

Cole, Henri.

[Poems. Selections]

Nothing to declare : poems / Henri Cole. — First edition.

pages cm

ISBN 978-0-374-22292-5 — ISBN 978-0-374-71332-4 (ebook)

I. Title.

PS3553.O4725 A6 2015

811'.54—dc23

2014027448

Designed by Quemadura

Farrar, Straus and Giroux books may be purchased for
educational, business, or promotional use. For information
on bulk purchases, please contact the Macmillan Corporate
and Premium Sales Department at 1-800-221-7945,
extension 5442, or write to specialmarkets@macmillan.com.

www.fsgbooks.com
www.twitter.com/fsgbooks
www.facebook.com/fsgbooks

P1

Frontispiece: Collage by Henri Cole

FOR KYOKO MORI

Friendship is all the house I have.

CONTENTS

I

I I

I

The earth does not argue,

Is not pathetic, has no arrangements,

Does not scream, haste, persuade, threaten, promise,

Makes no discriminations, has no conceivable failures,

Closes nothing, refuses nothing, shuts none out.

WALT WHITMAN, "To the Sayers of Words"

CITY HORSE

At the end of the road from concept to corpse,

sucked out to sea and washed up again—

with uprooted trees, crumpled cars, and collapsed houses—

facedown in dirt, and tied to a telephone pole,

as if trying to raise herself still, though one leg is broken,

to look around at the grotesque unbelievable landscape,

the color around her eyes, nose, and mane (the dapples of roan,

a mix of white and red hairs) now powdery gray—

O, wondrous horse; O, delicate horse—dead, dead—

with a bridle still buckled around her cheeks—"She was more

    smarter than me,

she just wait," a boy sobs, clutching a hand to his mouth

and stroking the majestic rowing legs,

stiff now, that could not outrun

the heavy, black, frothing water.

FREE DIRT

My house is mine:
the choice of menu,
the radio and television,
the unpolished floors,
the rumpled sheets.

It's like being inside
a rolltop desk. I have
no maid who takes care
of me. Sometimes,
during breakfast,

I speak French with
a taxidermied wren.
There is no debt
between us. We listen
to language tapes:

Viens-tu du ciel profond?
Always, I hear a little oratorio

inside my head. Moths

have carried away my carpets,

like invisible pallbearers.

I like invisibleness,

except in the moon's strong,

broad rays. Some nights,

I ask her paleness, "Will I be okay?"

I am weak and fruitless at night,

like a piece of meat with eyes,

but in the morning optimistic again,

like a snowflake that has traveled

many miles and many years

to be admired on the kitchen pane.

Alone, I guzzle

and litter and urinate

and shout. Please do not

wake me from this dream,

making meals from discrete

objects—a sweet potato,

a jar of marmalade,

a bottle of sauvignon blanc.

Today, I saw a sign

in majuscule for FREE DIRT

and thought, We all have

chapters we'd rather keep

unpublished, in which we

get down with the swirl.

The little wren perched on my

finger weighs almost nothing,

just nails and beak. But it

gives me tiny moments—

here at my kitchen table—

like a diaphanous chorus

mewling something

about love, or the haze

of love, a haze that makes

me squint-eyed and sick

if I think too much about it.

What am I but this flensed

syntax, sight and sound,

in which my heart, not

insulated yet, makes

ripple effects down the line?

THE BEE

For Jamaica Kincaid

There's a bee
dying slowly
outside my
window.
He/she

makes this awful
buzzing sound,
which grows
longer as
the end nears,

I suppose.
The mysterious
process at work
within him/her
is disturbing,

like a warm

wet finger.

Usually,

when you hear

a bee,

the sound dissipates

as the bee

flies away,

but this is constant,

so constant I think,

Maybe this bee

is stupidly in love

with me.

Or the buzzing

is inside

my head

and will become,

over time,

a friend—

a new kind

that doesn't go away,

even after lots of sex—

my ear canal

growing receptive,

like a hard bud

to light,

or a vulva

to the perfect

relation.

Would we know

each other,

I wonder,

if our eyes met across

a crowded room?

I did not expect

to meet this bee.

What else

could love be

but lots of buzzing—

or hate?

LIGHTNING TOWARD MORNING

In a thicket of bayberry
sowed early in the last
century, I am thoroughly
camouflaged. Nearby,
piping plovers are breeding

in a nest of fescue;
they are a rare species
in these parts, with whistling
peep-peeps and fine black
rings around their necks.

Probably only
an examiner
could distinguish
a raccoon's bones
from my own.

Wind, rain, and salt—
with animal feeding
and insect infestation—
have accelerated
decay. "You cunt,

you are nothing,"
he yelped at me
in that lonely moonscape,
as he did at the others,
runaways like me.

After it was over,
he auscultated my breast,
wrapping the whiteness
in burlap, my mind
a blown dandelion pod.

They are closer now,
wearing protective gloves,
boots, and coveralls,
a greenish wall
of sea tomatoes

impeding their cadaver dogs.

Overhead, a helicopter

films the area as divers

search west along

the causeway,

where in summer,

toward morning,

lightning falls

straight down

to the earth.

DANDELIONS

In the dream,

a priest said

it was time

to be entirely

adult.

Mother was bedridden

because of diabetes,

and her hands

had been

amputated.

Still, it was Mother

and not some creature

with a lolling tongue.

"Thank you for

the presents,"

she said kindly.
"Come back soon."
But the elegant
priest lingered,
demanding,

"Tell me
what you believe,"
as if it were her time,
though it plainly wasn't.
When he repeated,

"Tell me what
you believe,
woman,"
I grew
afraid

and went inside
my head, where I can
nearly always find
some dandelions
hugging the turf

with those silvery gray

stems and lemony

blossoms

that transform

any landscape,

and then I heard

Mother lifting her stumps,

where the hands had been,

telling him, "I believe

in these living hands."

SPHERE

For Harold Bloom

"Sir, I don't have no black tea," the waitress replied,

so I ordered Black Label instead. It was summer and the fragrant

white flowers of the black locusts had awakened, like faeries or

   obscure matter.

A black bear clothed in thorns made a mess of the bird feeder where

   hungry

blackcaps were a vision. And the black flies were biting energetically.

Billy died of the Black Death (I shouldn't call it that) and hovered like

   a winged horseman.

There's nothing so wrong as when young folks die. I smashed my bike,

blacked out, and got two black eyes. At the Mayo Clinic,

Daddy had his arteries cleared, praising the surgeon's fine black hands.

After he died, we called everyone in his black book and found

a black space that couldn't be lifted by impotent wings. Like me,

he was the black sheep. There were struggles. Once, driving near

   Black Mountain,

he blurted, "There ain't nothing so good as stolen corn or
   watermelon."
His face was like a smiling black spider's. Questioning the earth
from which he came ("Son, you got mixed blood")—and that drew
   him back—
he cleared a way forward into the murky light. Beside the roadside
   blacktop,
a deer, with black diamonds in its eyes, lay in a bed of black pansies.
Around us, black ash and black walnuts made a velvety curtain.
Dead ten years, he visits me often, like a head behind bars, with that
   black temper
and black bile still coming out of his mouth, but tenderness, too,
   like black gold.
Did I love him back, I wonder? If I loved him with all my heart
and all my liver, why did I spit him into the river?

LINCOLN AT THE STATE HOUSE

Columbus, Ohio—April 29, 1865

People in the rotunda stood
around transfixed as the undertaker
unscrewed the walnut coffin
to make a slight adjustment
in the position of the body.

With eyes closed, eyebrows arched,
and mouth set in the slightest smile,
he lay on white quilted satin.
At the autopsy, he lay on planks,
across two trestles, as a doctor,

sawing the skull, removed the brain
down to the track of the ball,
then not finding it removed the rest.
Heavy rain washed over the train,
and bonfires lighted small towns

along the tracks. The war

had ended, but people only realized

what he meant to them

after he was dead. Six white horses

pulled the hearse—

built in Chinese pagoda–style—

before the throngs waiting

to say goodbye,

including thieves,

whose pockets bulged.

With guns firing, drums beating,

and soldiers treading a sad,

slow march, the great block letters—

LINCOLN—were unnecessary.

In the Capitol,

a plush carpet muffled

the shoe leather of visitors,

including the Colored Masons

and the Colored Benevolent

Association, who approached timidly.

The catafalque was
a low dais, covered
with moss and leaves,
exuding the same odor
as at the Soldiers' Hospital,

where invalids had drenched
the street with lilac blooms,
which the hearse wheels
crushed. As the blood
drained from his body

through the jugular vein,
a chemical—force-pumped
into the thigh—hardened it
into marble. His face shaved,
except for a tuft at the chin,

and his brain—a soft gray
and white substance—
weighed and washed,
he was dressed in a low collar,
with a small black bow tie

and ivory kid gloves.
The black under his eyes
spread throughout his cheeks
but was not erased. There were relics:
death-bed sheets cut into squares,

locks of hair snipped,
wallpaper scraped with pocket
scissors, and the candle stub,
which doctors had held
lighted near his scalp.

Though Edwin Booth begged
for his brother's body, it was sewn
into a tarpaulin, with a gun case
for a coffin, and buried under
a penitentiary's brick floor.

MOTHER AND CHILD

Her teats were fat as ticks and her udder was heavy.

A little pink poked out from her vulva,

and she grunted softly while making small defecations

all around the stall. Pacing, pawing, standing up, and lying down,

she was waiting for the cover of darkness,

but when she started to sweat, the baby—perfectly well-made—

came quickly, groggy and gleaming from her insides.

Rubbing him with towels, we bowed our heads

at the straw where he lay—yeasty and squinting at us—

already alone in the bright landscape

and calling to mind remnants of defeated armies,

fleeing slaves, and refugees herded across

all the borders of the earth.

WAR RUG

The pony and the deer are trapped by tanks,

and the lady with the guitar is sad beyond words.

Hurtling across the sky, a missile has mistaken

a vehicle for a helicopter, exploding in a ball

of white flame. Upside-down birds—red specks

of knotted wool—glow above the sideways trees.

Hidden among plants, a barefooted boy waits—

like the divine coroner—aiming his rifle at something,

enjoying the attentions of a gray doggy, or maybe

there's a bullet already in his head.

HAND GRENADE BAG

This well-used little bag is just the right size
to carry a copy of the Psalms. Its plain-woven
flowers and helicopter share the sky with bombs
falling like turnips—he who makes light of other
men will be killed by a turnip. A bachelor,
I wear it across my shoulder—it's easier to be
a bachelor all my life than a widow for a day.
On the bag's face, two black shapes appear
to be crows—be guided by the crow and you
will come to a body—though they are
military aircraft. A man who needs fire
will soon enough hold it in his hands.

NOT A HAIR OF YOUR HEAD
SHALL BE HARMED

These hairs that the wind used to caress on my nape

fall from my brush now.

Let them float across the gardens like ropes

that once fastened Gulliver to Lilliput

or those silk walls that entangle insects.

Soon the rain will trample them into soil

or the birds will gather them up: straw or hair,

it's all the same to them, and man himself

has fabricated lampshades and soap

out of his own body. Don't worry—

"Not a hair of your head shall be harmed"—

nor shall the dead flakes of skin, the dormant neurons,

the dark ditches of memory.

Nor the loved and hated words of Hamlet—really just sounds

but no less resilient than these hairs

dispersing in a current of air.

Claire Malroux (translated from the French)

ENLIGHTENMENT MEANS LIVING

Writing this absorbed,

I realize that the words

are spilling all over

my legs, and I ask,

"Hey, what's this?"

When I go

to the window,

the words come too

and are just all

over the place.

It's as if my whole body

ceased to exist,

and I experience

the end of Henri

in an infinitude of words.

THE LONELY DOMAIN

"A Coffin—is a small Domain"

She had a bleeding vagina but no bosom
and a man's voice that barked, "Shut the fuck up,"
as she carried a carpenter's bench to the kitchen
and chose some boards from the yard. But I spoke
anyway, believing in words as the basis of people
living together.

                    She sat a long time making a sketch,
measuring the planks to mark them with a pencil,
and then all afternoon a saw wheezed
across the boards as her hands went back
and forth planing them, but even with a ruler
and chisel, it was hard to make the domain-end
wide enough for my shoulders. "Sorry about that,"
her voice vibrated.

                    Dogs bite strangers, wolves catch lambs,
lightning strikes trees, but strangely—without any
premonition—she quit her revenge, and the spell

was broken. "Let's talk," I said, sad and happy.

The kitchen smelled like a pine forest,

everyday thoughts that are my world

returned to me, sunlight was white

with misty distances, and I lived.

EXTRAORDINARY GERANIUMS

Eating a sugar sandwich, I sit at the kitchen table

admiring the geraniums outside the window,

their big heads as American as Martha Washington.

I grew them from seeds, and now the leaves are frilly like genitalia.

After so many sunrises together, they almost have faces,

with puffed-out mouths and throats, and when night falls,

they mix glamour with the gutter, like Paris or Rome,

but in the morning, they're themselves again, while birds hover

in the distance—hunting on the wind, using their tails to equilibrate,

pushing their shoulders forward and back to rise and fall.

I love this backstroking, or upstroking,

which the sparrows use, too, when they fly right in front of my car.

Lately, my vision has been graying a little at the edges,

but these geraniums, with their fragrant leaves,

and this gritty sugar sandwich make me feel my whole body

and my whole mind superimposed at once.

It's the opposite of self-obliteration.

If I think, Where am I? I immediately feel, I am here!

I I

Our bodies every seven years are completely fresh-materiald ∴ . 'T is an uneasy thought that in seven years the same hands cannot greet each other again.

JOHN KEATS, from a letter to George
and Georgiana Keats, September 17–27, 1819

HOTEL

My room is shaped like a cage.

The sun pushes its arm through the window.

But me—I want to smoke and make cloud images,

lighting my cigarette on the day's glow.

I don't want to work—I want to smoke.

(after Apollinaire)

CLEPSYDRA

After sustained winds,

a tidal surge, power outages,

waterlogged generators,

felled trees, and standing

on the roof,

I lay on the carpet,

letting the images

dart through me,

and thanked my life

for letting me be here,

while Albert mewed

and licked my eyelids

until they opened again,

like gold lamé

at a spa theater.

Then,

on the plasma screen,

water, fuel, and sewage

mixed

with debris,

a resilient rat blinked

at a flashlight beacon,

nurses carried

neonatal babies down

a dark stairway,

and fine sand painted

everything unnatural white.

When the wind howls

and a sea full of

compressed skulls

surges against

the windows,

we are all children.

It's the oldest timepiece—

liquid dripping in a tub

until the little clay vessel

fills and sinks to the bottom,

and a bare hand plunges in

to empty and

float it again.

STAGS

Sometime after the cherry branches fill with new green,

the first foaling begins, the fawns standing within an hour or two—

their reddish coats dappled with white—to drink from the lake,

tended by does, timid by nature but aggressive around their young;

and as green goes to red and brown, the plaintive intense stags—

having polished their horns against tree trunks and the earth—

indicate they are ready, and the battle of besting begins,

of pushing and butting with their racks and with all their strength,

until the victors gather their harems, jealously guarding them

from the defeated, who are done fighting, but alert to stealing a doe

that strays; now instinct is strongest, and the stags

think little of challenging humans. For this reason,

in October, we lasso and bind them (with difficulty,

given their bulk), and after the horns are sawed off,

the stags—weeping for what they have lost—flee to nearby groves.

This fantasy of finding something that's yours and making it your own—

as with darkness or light, as with romance—tells those

who set eyes on it that a momentous event is nearing.

SELF-PORTRAIT WITH RIFLE

For Claire Malroux

Why do they lie down

when I shoot them?

Such open,

willing obedience

seems to come

from an inclination

to serve. I wish

I could control

myself better,

but I am not grown yet,

and the mystery

of death means

nothing to me.

Perhaps it is better

to be feared than loved.

The deer do not

seem to grieve

because of what

they have lost,

but instead

seem to just

lie down on

the forest floor—

after sauntering

like little cathedrals

with antler-spires—

something whole

in between

man and God,

cloaked with red

hair to the membranes

of their eyes.

How strange

not to remember

even the blows

to their heads

that made them sleep—

to be so absorbed

by experience

and then to forget.

STAMPEDING BUFFALO

I was walking

home from the bank

and there was

a funeral

—white carnations,

twenty or so

mourners,

an intimate affair.

Later, when I

passed by,

only a large plastic

container for garbage

on wheels remained—

absence greater

than presence

had been.

At home, in a framed

photograph above

the mantelpiece,

buffalo plummeted

from a cliff,

tumbling

head over tail,

propelled forward

by their own

considerable weight,

while at the edge

one animal waited,

powerless before

the inertia

of the fall,

having seen

the others drop,

his hooves

clenching rock,

his shaggy coat

silhouetted against

white sky. On the sofa,

I lay listening

to a truck heave past,

and to the window-

panes rattle,

and to starlings

rearing up from a treetop,

swirling in the air

like script and then

descending again,

and to the mantel clock's

kind, minimalist

Don't be afraid.

THE ROCK

It's nice to have a lake to love me,

which can see under all my disguises—

where there is only animal survival

and the brutality of the unconscious—

and still love me and give me focus

and intensity, like a robin listening

to dirt for worms (those birds have talents

I don't: flying around with one eye closed

and half their brain asleep).

               Alone,

I like to swim (with no goggles, cap, or board)

out where I can see, high up, the white cedars,

and beyond that only the della Robbia blue.

On the other shore, a white pelican sits

on a rock, and, sometimes, feeding him—

beside the sign that says: DO NOT FEED THE PELICAN—

I think about all the dogmas and traditions

that are like well-made beds, with fitted sheets

and tucked-in hospital corners, to die in.

On my rock, it's as if everything is lit from below

or from within. There's no hierarchy

with pelican, water, rock, cedar, sky, and me.

A sense that all's right with the world prevails there—

and some kind of rock language,

with crude dents pressing my flesh,

and little fishes kissing my submerged feet.

GELDING.COM

Bishop Jack Freeman

and the Lamp of Jesus

Indian Meadow Homeless

Outreach Ministry

are looking

for a new home

for one of the horses

boarding at

the prayer house

near Defiance.

Henri is a gelding,

approximately eight to twelve

years old, in good

shape, well-fed

and cared for.

Because of an accident

he had prior to

coming to the ministry,

he cannot

be ridden.

However,

this injury

does not affect

his ability

to pull a load.

SARDINES

Cutting a slit

from the throat

to vent

and pulling out

the innards;

rinsing and stuffing

the insides with lemon

and thyme; wrapping

the flesh in paper-

thin prosciutto

to keep it

from falling apart;

then creating

a little oil slick

to fire them up,

like naked figures

harbored in my bed,

I think, I must

draw a veil

over the past.

I must

feel nothing

in connection

with it. But then

standing there,

eating forkfuls

like white violets,

pondering

a sky dark

with storm and rain,

I also think,

If I were

a little sparrow,

I'd fly

straight to him.

THE BOAT HEADER

I saw you

unexpectedly

on the street today.

Though it was midday,

your eyes were dilated.

You seemed

almost electrically

charged with thought,

with an increased

speed of speaking,

"I garden, I grill meat,

I prowl the bars."

But I was having

difficulty listening.

Your teeth were growing.

A muscle

spasmed against

my diaphragm;

I needed

a bag of ice.

Still, I could see

those rooms

with perfect clarity:

the coat rack

and bureau,

the dinner plates

with congealed meat,

the flea-market Piranesi,

and the long mirrors,

like camera lenses,

freezing us

as the boat header

gave you his final

thrusts, preparatory

to the cutting-in.

DANDELIONS (II)

He drew

these dandelions

during one

of the days

when the only

solace

was derived

from the labor

of getting

the white stems

and blurry seed heads

just right. *Nobody there,*

the new disease

announced

with black-tie gloom,

nobody there,

after he'd succumbed.

Sometimes,

sleeping soundly

is almost

unbearable.

"Please take

care of me,"

he asked,

as they put

his crayons

with his wallet

in a box

by the stove.

In the distance,

beyond the tulips,

an insect chorus

droned,

We beat you up;

we beat you up.

ANIMA

After he came back,

I accidentally

made the sound

that meant I

belonged to him

and felt it

to be true.

It was a warm type

of feeling that would

have been unwise

to have outside

at night, but suddenly

it seemed I would

not be outside

ever again,

where there had been
no time—just alive, or not—
in the shadows.

Now, there was
this new thing,
and, by day,

the sun accentuated
the feeling.
Then, in the moment

before it happened,
I thought, But I belong
to him.

Nevertheless,
it happened—
I died.

Though even dead,
some of me stayed
in bed with him

and couldn't

believe it.

Just let me be

here forever,

it thought,

I'm not done.

DOG AND MASTER

Consider the ermine—

territorial, noxious, thieving—

its dense fur whitening

when light is reduced.

Mesmerizing its victims

with a snake dance,

killing with a bite to

the back of the neck.

Born blind, deaf, and toothless,

the male is called a "dog,"

a roamer, a strayer,

a transient. But huddled

in my arms for warmth,

with my fingernails

stroking his underbelly,

he forgets his untamable
nature. His rounded
hips shiver like mine.
In folklore, he holds the soul
of a dead infant; and in life,

he prefers to give himself
up when hunted, rather
than soil himself. This is
civilization, I think, roughly
stroking his small ears.

But then, suddenly,
I'm chasing him around
the dining room screaming,
"No, I told you, no!" like two stupidly
loving, stupidly hating

creatures in a violent
marriage, or some weird
division of myself,
split off and abandoned
in order to live.

THE PARANOID FOREST

After a bout

of pneumonia,

he was searching

for something different.

It was rainy season;

a plague

of mosquitoes

had descended.

Eating ramen noodles

and fried eggs,

he'd acquired

a drug-addicted look.

Stung by fire ants

again and again,

wearing the moldy clothes

a little monkey

had peed on,

and grasping a machete

to cut through brush,

he let the frayed leash,

cinched at his wrist

to 250 pounds

of apex predator,

go where it wanted

(except down where refugees

had planted soybeans

and sunflowers),

his torso never

far from the cat's

as he took the same

steps it did,

its solemn eyes

turning around intermittently

to illuminate the forest,

like chandeliers.

Some men are afraid

of soldiers, some of their telephone

wires being tapped. Because

he had a secret,

he was afraid.

Birth, sex, sickness, death:

he was finished with them,

he thought, so one day

he disappeared into

complete silence

somewhere off the grid,

walking a big cat,

whose testes dangled

like a man's.

Still, the demands

of his secret were too great,

something not him still in him,

tethering him to a past,

which burned implacably

with the force of the sun.

THE CONSTANT LEAF

For Helen Vendler

I wish my father was here.
His features were calm and striking,
even when his breaths were horrible.

Remote pale yellow sunlight
behind a screen of clouds.
Landscape in darkness.

Rain comes straight down
in dense strands that cover
the street with rain froth.

The trees are so full it makes everything
seem constant but fragile,
as if any moment could be the last.

All the news is the same news:
somebody bombing somebody,
somebody cheating somebody,

somebody hurting the one he loves,

so we talk about forgiveness

in a low-key unabashed way:

forgive me for the errors of my youth;

forgive me for the fatal, incurable

virus that caused your blindness;

forgive me for the Stinger that blew

up your tenement. The wind

tears a power line from a pole,

sparking a transformer,

and the brick pavement is saturated

like mud. When I close my eyes and hold

my breath, I can stay in one place,

detoxifying experience like a kidney.

It's strange how the past holds on to us,

how the rapture of the lonely shore

is agreeable only if we can

at any moment escape it,

and how the night feels

so indispensable, soothing.

On the television,

at the white-domed Capitol,

a white man in a white room

lifts his glass of white wine.

I'm always searching the faces

of strangers for a friend.

ACKNOWLEDGMENTS

For their encouragement, I want to thank the editors of the following publications, where these poems, sometimes in different form, were originally published.

The Atlantic: "Gelding.com"

Little Star: "The Paranoid Forest"

The Harvard Advocate: "Lightning Toward Morning"

The New Republic: "The Constant Leaf," "Not a Hair
of Your Head Shall Be Harmed," and "Stags"

The New York Review of Books: "Dog and Master"

The New York Times: "Clepsydra"

The New Yorker: "Sphere"

The Paris Review: "Dandelions," "Extraordinary Geraniums,"
"Free Dirt," "The Rock," and "Self-portrait with Rifle"

Poem-a-Day (Academy of American Poets): "The Boat Header,"
"Hand Grenade Bag," and "War Rug"

Poetry: "Dandelions (II)"

The Threepenny Review: "City Horse" and "Sardines"

Salmagundi: "The Lonely Domain"

Slate: "The Bee"

The Yale Review: "Mother and Child" and "Stampeding Buffalo"

I would like to record my thanks to *Poets & Writers*, the Liana Foundation, and John and Susan Jackson for an award that was of great importance to me while writing this book.

This work was also supported in part by the Radcliffe Institute for Advanced Study at Harvard University.

Finally, I wish to record my thanks to Blue Mountain Center for its hospitality and solitude during invaluable residencies.

A NOTE ABOUT THE AUTHOR

Henri Cole was born in Fukuoka, Japan, in 1956. He has
published eight previous collections of poetry and received
many awards for his work, including the Jackson Poetry
Prize, the Kingsley Tufts Poetry Award, the Rome Prize,
the Berlin Prize, a Guggenheim Fellowship, and the Lenore
Marshall Poetry Prize. His previous collection was *Touch*.
He lives in Boston, where he is a fellow at the Radcliffe
Institute for Advanced Study at Harvard University.

Printed in the USA
CPSIA information can be obtained
at www.ICGtesting.com
LVHW091148150724
785511LV00005B/617